In the Windy City the snow is falling down, and the chilly air is swirling all around.

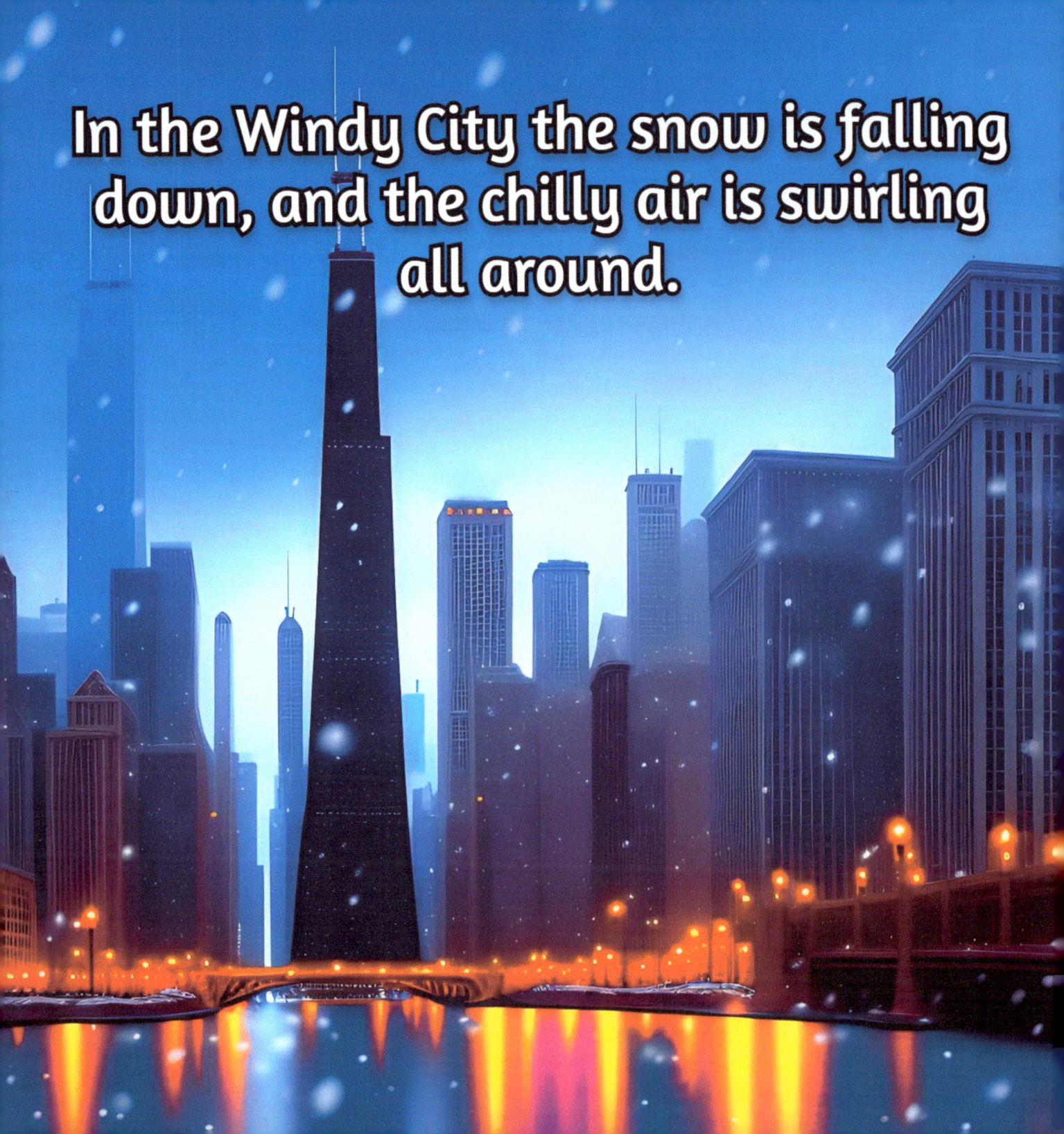

But the streets are buzzing with Holiday Cheer, as Christmastime is finally here!

The shops on State Street are all aglow, With twinkling lights and windows full of snow.

In Millennium Park, children marvel at the tree. So festive, bright, and grand to see.

The Christkindlmarket is a sight to behold, where Christmas themed treats and warm drinks are sold.

A light dusting of snow covers the Bean, and nowhere in sight can a sad face be seen.

Ice skaters glide and twirl with grace,
Downtown Chicago, a magical place.

Macy's windows dressed up with glee, a festive scene for all to see.

Lincoln Park Zoo, Oh what a view!
The sparkling lights will dazzle you.

Navy Pier all decked in lights. A magical wonderland of Holiday sights.

At Wrigley Field, the snowflakes fall.
A quiet stillness, no one plays ball.

WRIGLEY FIELD

HOME OF THE
CHICAGO CUBS

But we look forward to springtime with excitement and glee. For the crack of the bat, and the Cubs' victory!

Come Visit Santa in Hyde Park's Downtown. Where Holiday Magic can always be found.

Head to Ghirardelli Chocolate when the winter winds blow. Sip some hot chocolate nice and slow.

Horse-drawn carriage, a sight so rare, rolls down Michigan Avenue with grace and flair.

With the hustle and bustle of the city below, there's a sense of warmth that all shall know.

At Cook County's Forest Preserve with sled in hand, race down the hills of a Winter Wonderland.

As night falls over the city, the skyline aglow, a most beautiful sight for all to behold.

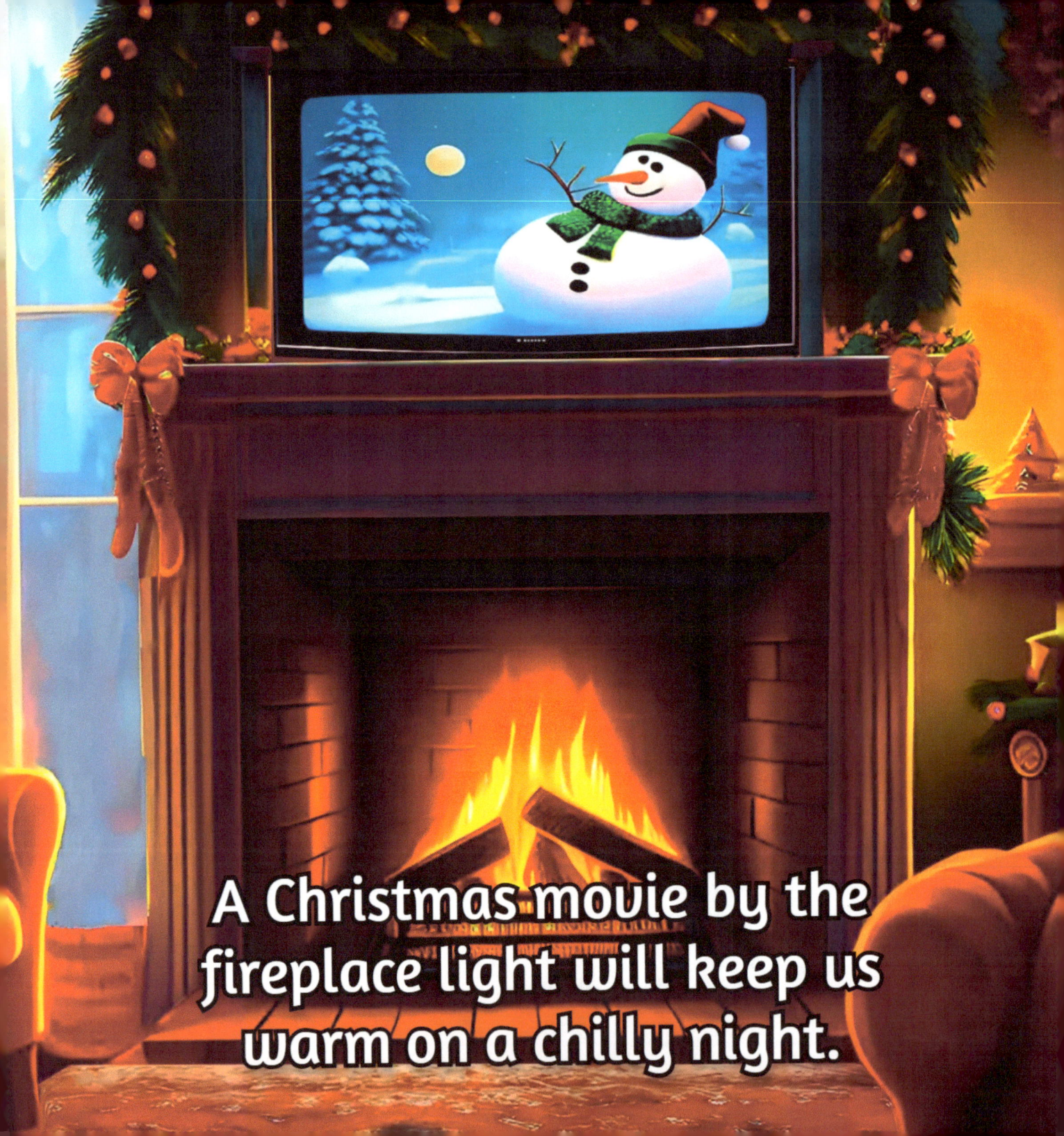

A Christmas movie by the fireplace light will keep us warm on a chilly night.

Leave out milk and cookies for Santa's delight, hoping he will come on Christmas night.

And on Christmas morning we rush to the tree, to find Santa left presents for you and me!

So if you're ever in Chi-Town at Christmastime, You'll see that its beauty is truly divine.

Merry Christmas
from
CHICAGO

www.ingramcontent.com/pod-product-compliance
Lightning Source LLC
Chambersburg PA
CBHW041722040426
42447CB00025B/209